LearnEnglish WithAfrica

Learn English With Africa

B1 Short Stories in English

(Vol. 1)

Intermediate Level

By
Thandi Ngwira Gatignol

CONTENTS

FOREWORD

This is a nice collection of eleven intermediate short stories that are fairly easy to read and understand. The stories are set in Africa and they feature a wide range of thought-provoking characters and themes.

The vocabulary might challenge you but do not give up! The more you read, the more you will understand. By the end of the book, you will see a noticeable difference in your level of English.

Tips for getting the most out of a short story

First, pay attention to the meaning of the story before focusing on vocabulary or grammatical structures.

Then, read the short story again and ask yourself the following questions: 1) What is the story about? 2) Who are the characters and what are their motivations? 3) What is the difference between the beginning of the short story and the end?

Lastly, write down interesting words, expressions or grammatical structures so that you can review them later. You will thus build your vocabulary and improve your English grammar in an active way.

I hope that this first collection of intermediate short stories meets your expectations and fosters your own creativity.

Thandi Ngwira Gatignol, Founder and Author (Learn English With Africa)

A Job for Joe
(with Vocabulary for Talking About Jobs)

Today is his lucky day. He finally has a job offer. It is true that when hope is gone, something unexpected happens and your dream finally comes true.

"Congratulations my son," his mother told him on the phone. "I knew this day would arrive. I am so proud of you."

His father did not say anything. He just held his hand for what seemed like ages. It has always been like that between them. Silence is the best expression of their love.

Joe knows that his family has been worried about him for a long time even though they have never told him. Two years on the job market is not easy and unwanted questions from random people were not helpful to get him out of his predicament.

How was the interview? Does Joe finally have a job? How old is he? When is Joe going to look for his own house? When is Joe getting married? Does Joe have a girlfriend? Is Joe an engineer or a doctor? Did you say that Joe was an architect? Joe is a surgeon, isn't he?

Good Lord! Those questions were annoying but he now knows what he is going to say to those people now.

"I'm the Deputy Manager of Wellington Farming Enterprises."

He can now start thinking seriously about his future. Of course, he will be able to find a small house. A bedsitter will do in the beginning and he can think of getting something bigger when he has saved enough money. He is not in a hurry to start a family of his own though. He has so many things to learn and this would not be fair for his-to-be wife. Besides, weddings are so expensive nowadays.

He checks the email again. It is true. He really has a job! His status has changed from jobseeker to future employee of Wellington Farming Enterprises. His Public Administration Bachelor's degree will now come to good use.

He remembers the interview. The only man in the four-member panel asked him what his personal qualities were. He told him that he was responsible, caring, demanding, empathetic, open-minded and good with animals. He thought that they would ask him many questions about his educational background. He did not study Agriculture at college level so he does not understand why they picked him for this job. Perhaps there is something that they saw in him that he is not aware of.

His siblings are happy for him. They have already asked him for video games and sneakers.

"Your first salary will be for us," they said without ambiguity. He will indulge them.

He laughs. He imagines going to the Human Resources Manager and getting his first pay check. Maybe the money will be directly deposited into his account. Maybe he will receive it in cash. The thing he is so sure of is that he will buy a set of sparkling pots for his dear mother. He might also replace his father's battery-operated radio with an electric one. He can do wonders with the salary of a Deputy Manager. He is also going to buy himself a new suit. He needs to be smart when he is going to work.

Working on a farm was not his dream job but he thinks that one has to be grateful for whatever opportunity they are given in life. Financial independence is important and he no longer wants to rely on his parents for upkeep money. He can start small but his career will be big. Who knows? He might end up as the General Manager of Wellington Farming Enterprises.

Whatever the job requirements are, he will do them with diligence and dedication. He will be punctual and committed and he will not act in an irresponsible manner. He does not want to waste this opportunity. He knows just how lucky he is. Many of his friends are still looking for jobs. The job market is saturated and he wonders if his younger brothers and sisters will have the same opportunities as he has now.

The following morning he goes to his workplace. It is a modern farm with new farming methods. They grow different types of crops like tea and maize but they also have some livestock. Joe will be responsible for paperwork both locally and regionally.

He asks if he can tour the farm. It is impressive and he feels that he has made the right choice to go and work there every day. It is only when they go and see the fields that he sees the cat. No, they are two cats, maybe three. Dear Lord-he is allergic to cats! He cannot work there. He has to turn the offer down. As they get nearer, he starts to sneeze and cough uncontrollably. The managing team understands. It is not the first time they have seen this.

Joe is despondent. His parents and siblings will be so disappointed. He will have to start looking for another job. He mentions this to the man on his right:

"Sir, I guess this is the end of everything. I can stand the stench of cow dung but I cannot control the way my body reacts to cats."

No, Joe doesn't have to worry. His air-conditioned office will be far from the cats and he will never see them again, the man says. It was hard finding Joe in the first place, wasn't it, and they do not want to let him go so easily. Young men no longer want to work in remote areas, they add. No, Joe, doesn't have to worry about the cats. They will not be a nuisance. Joe does not have to worry about anything. This is not a problem at all.

Back home, Joe still cannot believe his luck. His salary is beyond his dreams. On top of that, he has benefits that he never would have thought of getting with a job in the city: a company car, a furnished house, medical insurance, car insurance and paid holidays! His job will be demanding and he likes challenges. On top of that, there will be plenty of opportunities for his career to grow. Wellington

Farming Enterprises has ten farms in the entire country and they want to acquire some more.

When he goes to bed that night, he dreams of his future job and nothing can make him happier. Joe is a lucky young man. Joe has got a job, finally!

Uncle John Has Come to Stay

(with Vocabulary
for Talking About Families)

Uncle John arrived on a cold Monday morning.

He looked like the beggars we always met outside the PTC when we went to do our weekly shopping. He had the same battered look, the same nauseating stench, the same aimlessness that brought out our restlessness and gave us permission to judge, chuckle or taunt as our moods allowed.

"Uncle John has come to stay," my father told us in the solemn voice he used when talking to other adults.

"Greet your uncle," my mother asked and we did though we made sure to wash our hands with Dettol as soon as we went back into the house.

We giggled as we described Uncle John to the maid: "We're not joking anaMbewe. Go and see for yourself outside!" She came back in stitches, laughing so hard that we joined her until our bellies hurt and we couldn't laugh anymore.

"Is that your *father*'s brother? Really? You must be pulling my leg."

"We're telling you the truth anaMbewe. That's his real brother. Same blood, same womb!"

"What *happened* to him?"

"We…hic…hic…don't know…hic, hic, hic," we said in between hiccups. "He just turned out that way. My father says Uncle John was daft at school, hi, hi, hi."

"Noooooo. This is not the way things are done. You know what kids? That man should just have stayed where he was. Why did he come here? As if Daddy doesn't have enough problems already!"

We also invited our friends to come and see our uncle from the village and loved their reactions. "*Aise*, that one should just choose a spot outside Limbe PTC. Why does your mother even allow him to sit on *your* verandah? Are you sure he is your uncle? Be careful *Aise!*"

In fact, Uncle John was allowed to enter our house only after he had taken a shower in the Boys' Quarters. He was given some old clothes and ordered to burn his tattered ones in the rubbish pit outside. They also shaved his head to prevent a lice infestation and gave him *pata-patas* and Vaseline for his cracked feet.

You must be asking yourselves why Uncle John had left the comfort of his village to come to our house in town and brave our ridicule.

Well, where do I start?

His was a common story. A dead wife after a long and soul-shattering illness, five under-five children, no woman to look after them, Gin sachets day in and day out, helplessness, more helplessness and then flight.

So where were his children?

Where were his children? *Where were his children?* He didn't know! At least he had a roof over his head! He didn't mind sleeping on the floor in my brother's bedroom as long as he had somewhere to live. Anyway, we all knew that he didn't have any reason to complain. I mean he had no dust; he had clean blankets, clean bedsheets and a pillow, come to think of it. My brother *had* reason to be unhappy. He sulked for weeks after Uncle John's arrival until his anger had to be placated with a new pair of sneakers.

We didn't know when Uncle John would leave so we took advantage of every opportunity to make fun of him when our parents were not around. We laughed at his rough village manners. We imitated the way he ate *nsima*, taking full handfuls of the thick white paste, dipping it into the relish, stuffing the mixture in our mouths and swallowing it in one single gulp. We pretended that we didn't know how to use a flush toilet. We watched TV the way he did, staring at the device and commenting on the pictures all the time. We didn't know if he knew that we were mocking him but he never reacted to our jokes in a negative way.

Two months passed and he still hadn't left. My father said we had to give the man some time. He had been through a lot of hardship, we couldn't expect him to pick up the threads of his life in such a short period of time.

Another four months passed and Uncle John showed no signs of leaving.

"Uncle," he said, talking to my father, his younger brother. "Uncle, life is tough in the village right now.

Please bear with me. I will try to find a job and save a little money so that when I go back, I will have some cash to start with."

My father relented.

To keep his promise, Uncle John found a job as a night guard (my brother was delighted :-))). Uncle John worked every day of the week from five p.m. to six a.m. He slept the rest of the day and only woke up for quick baths and meals. He soon bought himself a bed and asked if he could put it in the Boys' Quarters.

My mother agreed and told anaMbewe to move out. She would be sleeping in our bedroom (we were not happy but my brother was) but we knew that it wasn't our maid's fault. Poor anaMbewe. She had been kicked out without ceremony.

We doubled our barbs at Uncle John (well, he had asked for it) and he continued to act as if he didn't care (maybe, he really didn't...) until after eight months he announced that he was getting married.

He had found a widow not far from the place he worked. Did my father mind if he could bring NyaNyirenda (the widow's name) to the Boys' Quarters? She would make no trouble. Anyway, it was just a temporary solution. Soon, they would both be on their way to the village. City life wasn't for them. Could my father lend him some money to help him settle his future wife in his humble abode (the Boys' Quarters)?

My father agreed; my mother didn't; our opinions didn't count; my father gave Uncle John the money he needed and in no time, NyaNyirenda, mother of three, was now a member of our family. Uncle John was now a proud father of eight children, five in the village and three in the city. He couldn't wait to add another child to this horde.

There was only a slight problem: there wasn't enough money for school uniforms and exercise books. Could my father lend him some Kwachas for that? He would pay off all his debts at the end of the month.

My father kept this new request as a secret. My mother was blissfully unaware of it. Uncle John got his way without a struggle. Everyone was happy.

Two years passed and Uncle John was still with us. His wish about a fourth child in the city had been granted. He was over the moon. He would go back home soon, he reassured us, it was just a matter of time and funds. *Why was he drinking away his money then every weekend*, my mother asked quietly. Why was his brother's wife not minding her own business? Be careful Auntie, remember where you came from! *Why were his kids coming to eat with us every day when their father had a job?* Why not, his brother was a General Manager! Did she want to eat the money alone? Did she know how their parents had suffered just to send his younger brother to school? Why would she be the only one to enjoy the fruits of that labour?

A year later, Uncle John was elated when he was blessed with yet another child. He now had double digits children. It was reason to celebrate with his friends.

"Enough!" my mother said. " Leave my house, you have taken advantage of my kindness and hospitality. Where are your other children by the way?"

"NyaMoyo, shut up!" Uncle John waved an angry fist at her.

My mother shut up; my father shut up; who could blame them?

Uncle John stayed with us for two more years until my father found a job in South Africa. This was a God-sent gift really.

We left in the middle of the night when Uncle John was still at work and his wife and seven children were still asleep. A friend of my father's came to fetch us. In our hands, we carried four suitcases and a travelling bag. AnaMbewe bid us goodbye as she walked towards her home village.

The Timetable
(with the Future Tense)

I'll do it," I said and he smiled.

"You're very brave Hilda," he said. "Everything will be all right. Don't worry. I'll call you as soon as I reach the airport. I have to go now. My plane leaves in two hours' time. I'm flying to Johannesburg first."

He planted a lingering kiss on her forehead and then headed towards his car. She waved him goodbye and entered the house. *Ana*Banda was waiting for her in the kitchen.

"Madam, I'm going to the market to buy some vegetables and meat for tonight's meal," she said in her endearing singsong voice. "I'll be back before five."

"All right, thank you for letting me know. You can also buy some bread and butter. I will cook some rice while you are away."

"OK Madam," she said. "See you later."

"See you."

Hilda drank a glass of water and braced herself for the next action. She was finally going to see the surprise that Mike had supposedly left for her. It was not a present, he'd insisted. It was more than that. It was something that she would remember as long as she lived. It was a token of love.

"You'll hate it the first time you see it but you'll learn to love it. After some time, you'll never let it go."

Well, as you can imagine, she had not known how to react to this news. It wasn't Mike's style to be so enigmatic.

"What is it?" she asked him one more time.

"A timetable."

"A timetable?"

"A timetable. It will help you to take care of yourself. Just spend some time with it."

She saw it as soon as she stepped into the dining room. There was also a cute notebook lying next to it. As she got nearer, she could make out some pens, markers, a ruler and a pencil. Many ideas rushed into her head. What was she supposed to do with all that?

First of all, the timetable wasn't a proper one. It was blank on top of it! She didn't have time to play with colourful pens and pencils like a child. She had better things to do!

"I'll have nothing to do with this," her inner voice bellowed loudly in her head. "I'm reading a book this evening as I initially planned. Why should I be fiddling with a silly piece of paper when I can make better use of my time? The best remedies for life's woes are the ones we discover through personal experience," she told herself firmly.

She made for the living-room but found herself thinking about Mike's surprise. Perhaps there was something more to this 'token of love' than could meet the eye? She simply could not focus on her book.

After sometime of fidgeting and tossing, she went back to the dining room. She sat down on the nearest chair and picked up the little notebook.

She wrote a heading on the first page. Soon, words started to flow freely from her pen.

WHAT'S HAPPENING THIS WEEK?

Schedule

- This week, I have a day shift. Work starts at eight and ends at three.
- I have an appointment with the dentist on Friday at five p.m.
- The next basketball training session is on Saturday.

Special Arrangements or Plans

- I am seeing Josephine at her place after work on Tuesday. She has invited me for dinner. I am actually looking forward to seeing her.
- I'm welcoming Mike at the airport on Sunday. I can't wait to see him!

My Intentions

- I am going to take good care of myself.
- I am not going to read books that are not interesting. I will insist on quality and not quantity.
- I am going to go out for evening walks after work.

It did not take her long to write the above sentences. She then took out the blank timetable and filled it in with all the compulsory events on her schedule. As an after-thought, she'd decided that she would complete the same timetable with the rest of her tasks only after she'd done them. This would help to motivate her.

Her week went as planned. She used the timetable as a guideline and found out that she was not wasting time as she would have done without this precious tool. What would Mike think of all the things she'd been able to do for herself and for others in that short period of time? Surely, he would be impressed!

Soon it was time to meet him at the airport. He looked very happy when she set her eyes on him.

"How was your week darling?" he said, planting a long kiss on her forehead.

"Wonderful," she said. "And productive." She added. "I missed you."

"He smiled knowingly and took her hands into his.

"I missed you too. I'm glad I'm back home."

"Let's go," they said in unison and laughed their hearts out at this coincidence, heading towards the exit.

"This year will be wonderful, he said when they'd stopped laughing. "I promise you, this year will be a great one. We'll have one hell of a good time!"

"We will," I said. "We'll surely have one hell of a good time! I promise you too."

Those Whispers Were Not Meant for Me

(with Small Talk Vocabulary)

I am lost.

The ground is hot.

My lips are parched.

The sun is out again and I fear I cannot walk.

My shadow follows me, or am I the one following it? What is this place? There is no sound and no one in sight. I should have stayed at home.

No time for regrets. Regrets are for fools and I am not a fool. I will see my wife. My child will call me 'Dad!' and he will nestle in my arms—once again. My parents will still have a child. I am their child. I am a father and a husband, a colleague and a friend. I will see my home again.

My feet are betraying me. I am dragging them but they will not move. The pain is unbearable. I cannot move. I drop my bag. It is a burden. My body is betraying me. I fight the tears that will not come.

I sit down and take off my shoes. I put them on again. I hoist myself up. My wobbly legs pull me to the ground. I stay there.

Time passes.

The sun's fiery rays descend on me.

I cannot fight them.

I wait.

I wait.

I wait.

I see moving shadows. I see them. They draw closer. A baby is crying. There are men. There are women. They are shouting and I can hear them. I can hear them well. There is life in this place. There is life. The group of people gets nearer. The men, women and children are finally here. They stop.

"What's your name?" I am asked. A man is asking that question. I am surprised that he speaks my language. I cannot speak his.

"What's your name?" he repeats. I tell him. He tells me his.

He gives me water. The ridges on my lips start to disappear. I cry.

"Where are you from and what are you doing here?"

I tell him. He tells me. They are nomads. They move from one place to another, looking for food and water. They have been walking for days. Resources are getting scarcer.

My head is lifted. More water finds my mouth.

The child starts crying.

"He is hungry," he says, pointing at him. "My wife doesn't have enough milk," he explains, pointing at her. She smiles.

I smile.

The child is still crying. They let him cry.

Tomorrow, they will find food. They will also find water.

"We found this."

It is my bag.

I look inside. My passport is still there. My wallet is not gone. I pull it out and take out some cash. I give it to the man. He shakes his head.

"It's useless here. Keep it. You will need it after you are back on your feet."

He wants my watch though. I give it to him.

They hoist me onto the back of the camel.

We are leaving this place. I am safe. I have been saved. I will see my wife. My child will call me 'Dad!'. My parents will still have a child. I am a father and a husband, a colleague and a friend. I will see my home once again. I am safe.

The Decision

(with Vocabulary for Talking About Decisions)

She had made up her mind.

Not that she minded the consequences. She had got used to them anyway.

Her Maths and Biology teacher had told her something about her future. "Bright and promising," that is what they had said.

They had not been patronising. She had actually been surprised by their kindness, their soliciting tones, their soothing voices.

They had told her that she was clever; that she was talented; that she would make it to Chancellor College, only if she wanted to.

She just had to work harder, do her homework all the time and never be late for classes as she did, at least once a fortnight.

It was hard to believe them.

She knew that she wasn't doing enough to get good grades. She knew that she wasn't doing enough to wake up earlier so that she could arrive at school on time. She knew that she wasn't doing enough to make her parents happy. She knew that she wasn't doing enough to keep herself out of trouble.

The truth was she hated going to school. She didn't understand why she had to go to school. She didn't see the ultimate goal, the ultimate reason why she had to work so hard, getting bad grades all the time and continuing to go to the same place that made her feel so bad. They said that it was for her own sake, for her future. Did she want to become a cleaner or a housewife, they would ask. She thought there was nothing bad about those occupations as long as the people doing them had enough food and were happy.

She felt that school was a total waste of time and resources. This was a place where teachers always shouted at you and nothing good came out of it. This was a place where teachers always pointed out your mistakes; one didn't actually want to do any good. This was a place where teachers punished you, and kept on punishing you, even though you never changed, or at least they never got the changes that they desired in you. This was also a place where no one really protected you from those punishments. If a teacher decided to punish you for as long as he wanted, then you were in real trouble. To her, this place did not seem safe at all.

Mrs Ngwenya and Mr Moyo had not even mentioned her punishments. As if they didn't know!

She was known for getting at least one punishment every week. Teachers were always racking their brains to find ways of finally making her do what they wanted. She had already swept the whole school yard. Mr Gama, the Chichewa teacher, had once made her uproot a whole mango tree stump. The year before, she had cleaned the windows of all the Form 2 level (that wasn't funny). She had even been asked to stand up during English lessons for a whole term (a whole term!). That was ridiculous.

Each time a teacher asked her to come in front of the class during a lesson, her classmates would start laughing. A few would pity her. A lone voice would protest but the teachers never swayed from whatever decision they had taken.

She remembered about Mrs Ngwenya's impromptu meeting and her relief when she went out of the small room. No punishment! Nothing. She remembered about being stressed during that week, thinking that the whole story was a joke. In the past, no teacher had let her go so easily.

All what had remained from that meeting were their words. Kind words, not hurtful words. Uplifting words, not demeaning words. Inspiring words, not hateful words.

She had thought about those words for days, day and night. Those words had followed her wherever she had gone. She had not been able to run away from them. They had been like a cloak of graceful redemption thrown above her head, covering her eyes, her whole face, but letting her see anyway. They had been like a blanket of protection, enveloping her and keeping her safe and nurtured.

Those beautiful words had gone straight to the very depths of her heart and their light had spread out to the rest of her being.

She had felt loved.

She wanted to hear more of those words.

It was her Geography teacher who noticed the change.

"Tadala, well done, you have done your homework on time."

"Thank you," she replied. She had learned not to take kind words for granted.

"Keep it up! If you do that during this whole term and continue, you will surely go to Chancellor College." This was even before the homework had been corrected!

It was her History teacher, Mr Manjonjo, who almost ruined everything.

"Why didn't you write the title of the essay in red as I asked? This is nonsense! Why can't you do as I say?" He crumpled the essay and threw it into the bin. "Write it properly next time."

"That was wrong," she told him.

"What? Am I hearing you right? What did you just say?"

"What you did was wrong."

"Who are you to say that? Have you lost your mind?"

"No, I haven't sir. What you just did was wrong."

"What did I do?"

"You threw away a whole week's work just because I did not write the title in red. That was really wrong."

"It doesn't matter. You're always getting into trouble anyway."

"No Sir, from now on I won't."

"We'll see."

"So what are you going to do about my essay?"

"What essay?"

"The one you just threw away."

Mr Manjonjo turned away and started writing on the blackboard.

She knew that he would never crumple any of her work again.

Don't Go There

(with Modal Verbs
and the Imperative Form)

"Don't go there."

"But you've been there."

"You can't go."

"Why?"

"It's not worth it."

"Sister, I don't understand. Surely, you must be hiding the truth."

The middle-aged woman stands up from the reed mat. She yawns and stretches her back. There is a cracking sound and then silence. She unwraps her *chitenje* and ties it again around her sagging waist. Her eyes wander to the kitchen and then back to the younger girl.

"I will tell you."

She starts walking with rickety steps, her shadow trailing her as she advances, slowly, and then a little faster, a little faster for she must reach her destination. She owes it to her sister who looks up to her. She owes it to herself.

Dragging her feet, she trudges. You think she will not make it, but she *will*. She **must.**

"Do you want something Sister? I will get it for you. You shouldn't be walking around with those legs."

"Don't worry Sister. You should rest after your long trip. I still have my strength, you know."

She lifts her feet. One. Two. Three. Four. Five. She stops. After a few interminable seconds she resumes her walk. Six. Seven. Eight. Nine. Ten. Eleven… She enters the small mud hut that looks like a chicken coop. It is the kitchen.

This windowless room is the place where she spends most of her time. This airless room is the place where she nurtures her family. This suffocating room is the place where she wastes her life, but she doesn't know it. The smoke she inhales daily, sitting by that makeshift fireplace, that smoke is poison for her. It draws out her breath by the second and shortens her life by years. She doesn't know this. It is difficult to imagine that she would like that fire, those charred pots, those broken wooden spoons, those rusty plates and pails. You can't imagine that.

When she comes out, she is carrying an old metal tray. In it, there is a bowl of groundnuts and two cups of steaming black tea that have already been sweetened.

"Oh Sister, you shouldn't have done that. Let me carry the tray."

The younger woman relieves her of the load. " Thank you," she says.

She follows behind, rubbing her red eyes and wiping away the black tears. Her clothes reek of smoke. Her face looks older, uglier. Her body is in pain, a pain that she masks with a smile. An old trick that has always worked for her and her friends. She reaches the mat and sits down, making sure not to spill the tea on the tray.

"Thank you Sister," the younger woman says. "You really shouldn't have done that.

"Don't worry, what are sisters for?"

There is silence.

The younger woman breaks it after some minutes.

"Sister, I'm sorry to talk about this again but why shouldn't I go there? Look at you Sister. You should go back there too; you would live much better abroad. What are you doing here, wasting your life in this God-forsaken place?"

"You really want to go there, do you?"

"Of course, I do."

"Then think carefully of what you will lose when you go there."

"Lose? Sister, lose what? What can I lose here? I'll be so glad to get rid of this poverty. Given the opportunity Sister, I want even think twice. Do you know what I'll do when I reach there?"

The middle-aged woman shakes her head.

"I'll burn all the old things from here to have a fresher start there!"

The middle-aged woman continues to shake her head.

"What will you do there? Do you have any plans?"

"I'll work Sister."

"Where?"

"I don't know Sister. There are plenty of jobs there. Any type of job will do for me. Any."

"Are you sure? Do you really mean what you are saying? Will any type of job suit you? Any type? Even a job that you wouldn't even consider having here?"

"Any sister, I'll be alright. Iiii Sister, you are asking too many questions, why?"

The older woman coughs and starts to say something. She is interrupted by a peep of chickens that strut past, pecking at the ground in an orderly way.

"Do you realise that you will have no family there?"

There is silence.

"Do you realise that people here will have no sympathy for you? They will think that you are enjoying yourself abroad all the time. You will have to buy their sympathy and love but for how long? How long can you buy people's sympathy?"

A fly lands on her cup and she shoos it away with an impatient hand. She continues her series of questions.

"Do you realise that you will be alone most of the time there?"

The younger woman answers: " Loneliness can be good sometimes."

"It is not the loneliness that you imagine," the older woman says, wincing as if she is battling some encrusted pain. " This loneliness is unimaginable. It is that type of loneliness that makes you watch television all day because you want to be in the company of others."

The younger woman stares at her, through her, past her. She sees herself in one of those huge well-furnished houses. "Why do they make their houses so big then?"

"Don't even dream of that. Do you think that cleaning jobs will get you such a house? The truth is that you will struggle there. You will suffer. You will cry all the time. You will spend evenings alone. You will be on your own during holidays. You will give birth alone and you will raise your children alone. You will do EVERYTHING alone. Is this the type of life you want?"

"Surely Sister, there must be some good sides to this life. I'll be so glad to escape the gossip here."

The older woman grabs her hand and rests it in one of her rough palms. "Listen."

"I am listening Sister."

"It's not a life for you. You have so much here; you just don't know it yet. We know the value of things when they are gone. You have so much here; you really have to understand that."

"I'm fed up of this life; I just want to go away."

"What can you do to make your life better here? Remember that you will never be able to retrieve what you will lose by leaving this place."

"I know."

"So why do you still want to abandon all your life treasures for unknown ones? Why?" The younger woman's hand is still in her palm. She presses it gently and continues speaking: " You will no longer exist as yourself there, do you know that? Those people will not be interested in your life, in your past, in your culture, in everything that makes YOU, do you know that? You will sit with one buttock on the sofa and stand with one foot outside the door. You will survive and not live. You will walk with a hunched back and speak quietly to avoid taking too much space, if you are allowed to speak at all!" You will learn to disappear and be a nobody." Her voice is firm and coloured with emotion.

"How can that be possible?"

"I don't know, but it is. I have seen it with my own eyes. When you are there, you will do your best to learn their ways but you will never be good enough for them and you will become too good for the people here. You will always be a copy there, do you understand that? A copy, a cheaper version of yourself. You may go there if you want but I think you will pay a huge price for that. You might not even come back."

The younger woman is startled. She doesn't know what her sister means. She wonders what it feels like to be a copy of someone, to live under the shadow of her former self, to no longer exist as herself, to lose her ambitions, to live a second-class life, to perform another person's script and not be able to achieve the desired goal, to lose her identity.

"Your life will be a perpetual struggle, a fight against time, a fight against prejudice, a fight against misconceptions. You will experience the type of despair you have never experienced here, I am telling you. Their lack of concern for you will make you angry, and then very angry, and then sad, and then very sad, and then desperate. They will give you medicine for your sadness. This medicine will take away your sadness but you will feel nothing else afterwards. I do not want you to go through that Sister. I do not want that. Depression, they call it. You will be at the hospital and they will rarely come to see you. They will not care if you pull through. They will not want to know your problems; they won't. You will gradually learn to fill your emptiness with objects that you don't need. Those objects will overwhelm you in no time and you will learn to get rid of them to make space for some more. You will be sick for home."

"Iiii Sister, how do people survive?"

"They are used to it. They are used to being mistreated themselves. Maybe they don't have a choice. Let me tell you one thing though Sister. If you still want to go there and go through all that, don't forget one very important thing. You are worthy. You have worth. You are capable of doing SO much with your life and no one can take away your dreams. Everyone is born with a purpose in life. We all have something to achieve so don't ever think that you have no right to live a dignified existence on this earth because someone else has said so. Always believe in yourself and in your abilities."

"What would you do if you were in my shoes Sister?"

"If I really had to leave, I would do so with a specific plan and purpose. I would not allow myself to be blown by the wind. The best thing to do would be to study and gain some real skills. Afterwards, I would come back. I would surely do because there would be absolutely no future for me there. I would prefer to struggle in my homeland and contribute to the development of my country, instead of wasting my life in some foreign land, wandering and drifting with no purpose at all."

Her eyes are clouded with unwanted memories. Memories about lonely childbirths and memories about lonely celebrations. She wants to forget the unsolicited advice and the unsolicited insults. She yearns for the time when she will no longer wake up at night, haunted by the taunts of teenagers who knew nothing about her life but decided to hate and hurt her anyway. She remembers the shell she was when she finally decided to go back home. She remembers how her children struggled to cope in their new land. She remembers how her relatives had changed, how she herself had changed. She remembers how she could no longer find the space she had left, despite momentous efforts to do so. She remembers the agony at realising that she could not find this space back. It was gone forever. She remembers wishing she had never left at all.

"Oh sister, what a life. I didn't know."

"How could you? You just saw the planes, the clothes, the phones, the money. You didn't see the desert inside. No material things can replace your home, do you understand Sister? Nothing can replace your real home. Why do we all want to leave? Isn't this land good enough for us? If we all flee, who is going to take care of it? Who, I ask, is going to take care of our bleeding land?" She grabs a corner of her wrapper and wipes the tears that are starting to well in her eyes.

"Let us take care of ourselves and our country. We deserve much, much better. Why do we let ourselves suffer in faraway lands when we have a beautiful land with plenty of resources, why Sister? We can't spend our entire lives begging and grovelling as if we have no dignity Sister. They don't give us their love and turn us into radicals. No Sister, we deserve much, much better than their love. We need to start loving ourselves."

Her eyes dart to the kitchen and she gives an impatient sigh. She stands and is momentarily surprised by the energy in her legs. She has so much to do, so many projects to realise. The future can only be better. She grabs the younger woman's hand and helps her to her feet. They walk together towards the mud hut to do what they know they must do. With powerful strokes, they bring down the shack, taking pleasure in felling the rickety walls. They laugh as they throw away the broken pots. They jump with glee as they remove the dirt, the twigs, the blackened fireplace stones, the rusty pails, the rusty plates. They don't care. They will have new ones. They will build a new kitchen that they deserve. It will be modern with ample windows and ample room, smoke will be chased out of their lives forever. They will be free, finally!

I Will Not Learn Under a Mango Tree

(with the Simple Past Tense)

Today is the first and last day of school for me this year. I do not want to learn under a mango tree. My friends do not want to learn under a guava tree either. Even our teachers are shunning the popular baobab tree. **'FLEE THE TREES IN THREES, I BESEECH THEE'**, our headmaster jokes about it, but we know that this is not a laughing matter. We stopped laughing about such things a long time ago. We will not laugh about this today.

Last year, 312 pupils in Standard 8 sat for their Primary School Leaving Certificate Examination (PSLCE). They were from 3 classes. Out of those 312 pupils, only 13 were selected to continue their studies in a government conventional secondary school. 33 others were lucky enough to get a place in a community day secondary school. A select few went to private schools, dozens dropped out of school altogether and the stubborn remaining ones came back here to repeat. As if this was not enough, 3 experienced teachers left for greener pastures and were replaced with 3 unexperienced ones. This year, I was supposed to start and finish my Standard 7. I did the first but I will not do the latter.

Before I go on, let me introduce myself. My name is Jack. I am the fourth-born child of Mr and Mrs Phiri. They are both from Dedza but we live in Salima now. I have two brothers and two sisters. My parents are small-scale farmers. They grow different types of crops such as maize and groundnuts that we mostly consume in our household. The little that is left is sold by my mother at the market when the days are good. My eldest sister also sells doughnuts in order to find money for buying school supplies and groceries such as salt, sugar and soap.

What are my ambitions? In the future, I would like to go to Bunda College to study Agriculture because I am very good at this subject. My teachers think I could easily become a doctor too. Who knows? I still have 6 more years to go before I start seriously thinking about such matters.

Today, I arrived at school in a jovial mood. I had everything I needed: a uniform, a new pair of shoes, 2 pens, a pencil with a rubber and a small container of soaked roasted maize. I was really looking forward to the notebook-giving ceremony too. I was eager to receive the clean and crispy exercise books and was planning to cover them with newspapers as soon as I got back home. I knew I would not get any textbooks because they always remained in the school library. There were too many pupils and those precious books would not be enough for everyone.

When we were at assembly in the school yard, a gust of wind, which came out of nowhere, sliced into the headmaster's speech and carried his words away into the blue sky. For a brief, recognisable and unforgettable moment, thick clouds of dust billowed over our heads. I could not see anyone at all as dry leaves swirled senselessly around us in a mad but consistent way. We waited for the dust storm to abate. When it did, the trail of disaster in its wake could not be described with simple vocabulary. We were speechless, dumbfounded, tongue-tied, voiceless.

The teachers ran about, checking if everyone was alright. Then one by one, they started calling out our names: *Mercy Chisale, Misozi Mbewe, John Kamanga, Kondwani Banda, Justice Chidothi, Jack Phiri, Victor Kamanga...*The list went on and on and we listened carefully in case we missed something, someone.

We waited for the dust to settle but it would not. The headmaster decided to resume his speech all the same. We waited to hear the thunder in his words but all that we grasped was the thunderous crash of the biggest and oldest mango tree in our school. It was where my classmates and I were supposed to sit that very same morning. Our **classroom** was gone! Our beloved classroom was gone!

We all stared at our former classroom in wonder and awe. The broken tree trunk was lodged between two rows of desks and the branches had spread out into different directions. The remainder of the original tree jutted into the air ominously. Our eyes could not believe what we saw. Our mouths failed to describe the scene that was right in front of us.

"There will be no school today," the headmaster finally announced in a deep solemn voice. He was trembling with fear, and anger, and pain. We stood there, not understanding his words, not understanding what he wanted to tell us.

"Go back home," he repeated. "Go back home to where you are safe," he said. "There will be no learning today, nor tomorrow, nor the day after tomorrow. Go back home until we remove this terrible thorn that is digging into our feet and tearing at our flesh. Let the birds and rodents reclaim their territory. **WE ARE HUMAN BEINGS AND WE HAVE A BASIC AND UNIVERSAL RIGHT TO EDUCATION**. My dear pupils, I want you to thrive and not survive. I want you to learn in a much better environment than we have right now. The 'school' we have here is a ***mockery***."

We listened and nodded. What a way to start our year! What would we do now? Where would we learn?

"My dear pupils, we will build ***real*** classroom blocks with the sweat of our hands because we are able to do so. When we do, going to secondary school will no longer be an impossible dream. When you have a thorn in your foot, you remove it yourself because it is you, and only you, that is feeling the pain. No one will do it for you."

I imagined what it would feel like to learn in a ***real*** classroom with ***real*** walls and a ***real*** roof! I imagined being free from distractions and impromptu visits of the wind and rain. I imagined passing my PSLCE with flying colours and preparing to go to boarding school. We could do it! We were capable of doing it! We were smart and strong!

Josephine, My Love

(with Vocabulary
for Describing Love)

I loved her the very instant I saw her, God knows I did. Josephine.

She was a beauty, and still is, though I haven't seen her in such a long time. I wish I could.

We met when I was fourteen years old. She was fifteen.

My parents sent me to my paternal home village last year in summer.

"This boy needs to toughen up," I heard my father tell my mother at the breakfast table. "He needs to see how other people live."

My mother did not really want to send me away. She rarely saw us during the day because of her job and holidays are a great opportunity for her to catch up on the duties of motherhood.

"We can go there together at Christmas. Everyone will be happy. He is too young to be sent off like that on his own. His friends are here. His whole life is here. We don't even know how they will look after him there."

There were many reasons why those holidays were important to my father. I couldn't grasp the true meaning of those reasons at the time even though my father tried to explain them to me. It was later on, much later on, that I understood those salient reasons.

It was tough for my mother to let me go. She wrestled with this issue for a long time. Why was I being sent there alone? Why couldn't I go there with my siblings? Why couldn't she come along with me? Why couldn't my father accompany me? Why couldn't my cousins from the village visit us?

In the end, she did let me go, half-heartedly. I was so disappointed. Secretly, I had hoped that I would be able to stay in the city. They were so many things to do that summer in Blantyre that I could not imagine wasting my life in some remote village with no running water and electricity. I felt like my father was punishing me for my poor performance at school that year. I felt like my father was abandoning me, giving up on me. With hindsight, I know this is one of the best decisions he ever took regarding my upbringing. It was a decision that came from a place of love.

Those holidays did change my life.

I saw Josephine the very first day I arrived in Bolero. She was passing by my grandparents' house and my cousin, Cecilia, chatted with her for a few minutes. I could barely make out her features but I knew that I had never felt that way before. I wanted to see this girl again, it was such an urgent need, it almost felt painful. That fleeting image would haunt me for days: her smile and soft laughter, her plump figure, her smooth skin that reminded me of ripe mangoes... I remembered everything about her.

I remembered her neat rows of pleated hair that glistened in the sun. I remembered her dimples, her disarming smile, her nonchalance, her everything. Her picture was so clear in my head, the clothes that she wore, the shoes that she put on, the words that she said! It was if I had been there to photograph each and every second of her existence because I knew that this would be the very last time I would be seeing her at such close range. The pictures I took in my head would keep me restless for endless days and nights.

I really wanted to see this girl again. It was almost a matter of life and death.

I had so many questions for Cecilia. Who was that lovely girl? Where did she live? Did she go to the same school as Cecilia? Could we go to her house together? Could we just see her again, one more time? One last time?

"That's your namesake," Cecilia teased me, her eyes gleaming with mischief. "Namesakes are meant to be with each other. Namesakes are supposed to love each other until death do them apart."

I didn't understand.

"Joseph, Josephine is your namesake, can't you see that? Joseph and Josephine! Joseph and Josephine! Joseph and Josephine! Joseph is in love with Josephine. Joseph and Josephine are in love..."

I laughed so hard and almost cried, it was too good to be true. I told Cecilia to shut up but she wouldn't. Deep inside, I wanted her to continue chanting those names. It made Josephine exist as a relevant being in my life. Whenever Cecilia mentioned that name, Josephine ceased to be immaterial. She turned into real flesh and came to life. She was my Josephine. Josephine, the greatest love of my life.

Josephine. Josephine, my love. Josephine, my true love. Josephine, my one and only. My beloved Josephine. My lovely Josephine.

I was in love. I was in love with Josephine.

I learned that Josephine was fifteen years old. She was the last born daughter of Mr. and Mrs. Mwafulirwa. She was a Form 2 student at Livingstonia Girls' Secondary School. She was a very smart girl (head-wise and fashion-wise). She had no boyfriend and, as far as Cecilia was concerned, she was not looking for one.

"Not even a handsome and intelligent boy from Blantyre?" I asked Cecilia hopefully.

Cecilia smiled sadly and patted me on my shoulder. "You're not the first person from the city that has ever come to our village. Others have failed before you. Having boyfriends is not Josephine's number one priority. That girl has big brains. She wants to become an engineer. Do you think she is going to waste her time with you? Why do you want her to be your girlfriend?"

"She is the most lovely and radiant person I have ever seen. I just want to know her better. I want her to be part of my life."

You can imagine what I did during those holidays to conquer Josephine's affection.

I wrote her fiery letters. I sent her little presents. I asked my cousin over and over again if she could bring Josephine to the house, even if it were for some mere precious seconds. I passed by the borehole several times a day, hoping that I would catch a glimpse of her silhouette as she fetched water several times a day. I rarely succeeded in my endeavours but when I did…God, it was one of the most satisfying feelings I have ever had. My heart felt warm for days on end and my headaches disappeared. I talked about her for days until Cecilia told me that it was about time I got over this girl.

"You barely know her," Cecilia told me one day. "She doesn't love you."

Was this true?

My cousins words hurt me.

Yet, the truth was stark clear. It was right there, in front of my eyes.

Josephine did not reply to my letters. She did not talk to me. She did not accept any of my presents. She did not smile back at me when I showered her with the warmth of my heart. Josephine rarely looked at me. I was insignificant in her eyes. I was a pure joke. I would never hold a special place in her heart. She would never reciprocate my love.

In the end, I finally accepted this truth, reluctantly. I decided to spend the rest of my holidays playing with my cousins in the bush and at the river. We hunted for mice. We swam. We made cars from fencing wire and we did mock orchestra bands. We went into the woods to fetch wild fruit that we shared with our little cousins back home. We loved seeing their reactions as we gave them the bounty. They would be playing *ndado* and as soon as they saw us, they would shout **"FRUUUUIIIIIT!"** and rush towards us to get their present.

It was always a wonderful moment. We would then roast dry maize and groundnuts and eat them while we talked about our day. We played from sunrise to sunset. Our days were eventful and I was sad to leave all this behind when it was time to go back home. I hoped Josephine would come to say goodbye. She didn't. I was not surprised. I knew that she was resolute in her choices. Josephine. Josephine, my love.

I have yet to see Josephine again. I haven't forgotten her. Cecilia regularly gives me news about my love (Yes, my love, my Josephine, my one and only). She still wants to become an engineer. Her dream is to be selected to the Polytechnic University where she can pursue a Civil Engineering degree.

"Josephine has great plans for our village," Cecicila wrote to me. "She wants none of this pointless suffering and hopelessness any more. She believes that when you really want something you can have it. No situation, however desperate it might appear, is written in stone. Things change and for the better, when we want them to, when we all want them to. Where there is a will, there is way. Josephine has a strong will."

I will always love Josephine. She will always have a special place in my heart. I want her to be the mother of my children. I want my children to call her Josephine 'Mum'. One day they will, surely.

People cannot understand why I love a girl who does not even want to look at me. They say that I am infatuated with her. Some even say that she put a spell on me. They say that I have changed quite a lot since I came back from the village. I pay a lot more attention to my studies. I help my parents at home. I am more respectful towards elders. It is true that I now think more about my future. I want to live with purpose. I am no longer drifting in this world like I used to. I have specific goals and dreams.

I want to live a good life. I hope I can live this good life with Josephine.

I can picture us walking and working in Bolero in ten years' time, fifteen years' time, twenty years' time… Together we will work at transforming Bolero, my home village. I swear that Bolero will have functional electricity, running water, good sanitation facilities, excellent schools and magnificent roads in my lifetime.

Bolero, our home village, will nurture our love. Josephine and I will take care of Bolero in return. I cannot wait for this to happen. I hope I could talk about all this with Josephine. I worry not though. Time will come. Time will come when I can talk and do all these things with Josephine.

I know I will always love this girl.

She is my true love.

We are a match made in heaven

I love Josephine. I really do.

I miss Josephine. I just cannot stand it.

Josephine, my love. I cherish you. I love you. I adore you.

You will always, always have a special place in my heart!

Things

(with Objects Vocabulary)

We saw the lorry way before our father did. It was filled with objects that we had never seen in our whole lives. The colours impressed us; the shapes beckoned to us. We longed to touch those mysterious things and hold them in our bosoms forever.

The vehicle advanced towards our house. It moved slowly, its metallic shine dazzling us, its ridged tyres making a way through the narrow path in a steady manner. Men, women and children lined the road, admiring its splendour. It was a rare sight.

We wanted to be near it so we ran alongside its belly, brushing our fingers against the hard metal. It was marvellous to feel the cold structure. It was heavenly to be in contact with this majestic creation.

Previously, the driver of the car (a woman!) had to stopped to ask us if we knew anyone who spoke English in the village. She was wearing sunglasses and a white cap.

"Of course!", my younger brother replied, dropping his ball onto the ground. " My father. My father speaks very good English. He is also our school headmaster. I will take you to him. He will be very happy to see you."

The other three occupants of the car had smiled and congratulated him for his good command of English.

"Where did you learn English?" A young man asked my brother.

"At school," he replied. " English is my favourite subject."

They asked to take our pictures and we posed and posed for the camera, shouting "Cheese! Cheese!" They clicked and clicked in our direction and we laughed our hearts out.

We couldn't believe our eyes when we saw the back of the lorry. They were many things but we did not really know their names. Derrick was sure he had seen a bicycle. Jack thought he had seen a TV set. I, myself, had spotted a plastic mirror.

It took about thirty minutes for the lorry to wade through the admiring yet bewildered crowd. When we arrived at home, my father was standing on the veranda. The noise had brought him outside. He took off his eye-glasses and peered at us as if that would make his eyesight better.

The visitors, two men and two women, got out the vehicle and shouted a hasty 'hello' to him. At that moment, my mother also appeared from behind the kitchen. Her wrapper was smeared with maize flour. When she saw the people who had come to her house, she covered her mouth in mock embarrassment. She smiled shyly at us before retreating back to the kitchen, no word escaping her mouth.

"Welcome, welcome," my father finally said. "Let us go inside the house and greet each other properly. I cannot let you stand outside like thieves. Let us go inside. Let us go to the living room."

The young man who had previously spoken to my brother insisted that he wanted to stay outside. It was hot and the yard was inviting.

"We like it here," he said, laughing lightly. "It is lovely, I must say."

"No, no, no," my father insisted. "You shall be received properly."

The woman who had been driving cast furtive glances at the lorry.

"Don't worry," my father reassured her. "I will entrust your vehicle to two big boys whom I have raised myself. I will make sure they don't touch a single object in that car."

The visitors still weren't sure if this was the right thing to do.

"Is it okay? Are you sure we can leave all this here?"

"Don't worry," my father repeated. "Everything will be alright.

The party finally entered the house when my two elder cousins, Mwiza and Gomezgani, arrived. The latter had two long sticks and they whipped whoever wanted to get near the lorry.

"Go away you good-for-nothing-children! There are no goodies for you here!" my cousins bellowed.

The curious children scattered in all directions as their mothers yelled at them too: "Come back you foolish kids! Why are you getting beaten for that nonsense? You don't even know what's in that car!"

The temptation was too strong though. Vehicles of such calibre never entered our village every day. Therefore, the kids came back but stood a few metres away from the car, watching hungrily, hoping my two zealous cousins would loosen their guard and let them have a peek at the hidden treasure.

There were two dining chairs on the veranda. I was asked to take them into the living room and place them next to coffee table. It was covered with the skin of a goat and it stood near our old green sofa and its pair of matching armchairs. There was a vase of plastic flowers on the sideboard. My father and mother smiled at us from a picture frame.

My brother was sent to buy four bottles of Coca-Cola and four bottles of Fanta. We hoped we would be able to have a sip. Christmas was so far away and there were no weddings to be held that year in the village. If only the visitors would leave some of their soft drinks in their tumblers.

My father let me stay in the living room exceptionally.

"You want to be a journalist, don't you," he said. "Sit here with me and take notes of what these people would like to tell me. It might be important and I don't want to forget anything. My memory is tricking me nowadays."

I was proud to be given this task. I rushed to the bedroom I shared with my four sisters and three cousins. I took a blue ballpoint pen and a piece of paper from my Arithmetic notebook which our teacher had given us at the beginning of the school year.

When I went back to the living room, one of the young men was introducing himself and his friends. His name was John and his friend's name was Steven. The young women were called Suzie and Alison respectively. I wrote down everything they said, asking them to spell their names because I was not sure how to write them. They looked at me inquisitively but never asked any questions.

Then it was our turn to introduce ourselves. My father said his name was Bright Nyirongo. He was a primary school headmaster. His wife was called Mary. She was a housewife. She looked after the kids, helped him in the fields and made sure he was a happy man. Steven and Alison laughed and my father continued to speak:

"This one here is Tawonga. She is twelve years old. She wants to be a journalist one day. Well, before you tell us the purpose of your visit, I would like to call my wife. She should also hear what you have to say. As the old adage goes, one head cannot carry a roof. We need to be together as husband and wife when important decisions are to be made.

I was asked to fetch my mother. She came after changing into a new outfit. She made sure to put on her favourite headscarf which she donned during special occasions.

She greeted the visitors, one by one, holding their hands firmly, kneeling, avoiding their eyes.

"Thank you for your visit," she said. "You are most welcome here. How did you leave your parents back home? Are they alright?"

"I guess they're doing ok. Anyway, they were fine when we left them," John chuckled, looking at Steven.

"That's good my son, that's good. Health should be cherished all the time. It is a gift we cannot ignore. I am happy that you left your old folks in good health. We must also thank them for letting you come all this way to see us in our humble village."

The visitors nodded, laughing silently.

My father asked my mother if the soft drinks were ready. She said my brother was not back yet.

"Give them some water then."

"Yes *Dada*," she replied and stood up to get fresh cold water from an earthenware pot that stood near her bedroom door.

"Tawonga, go and help your mother. Bring some groundnuts for our visitors to nibble; I mean for Steven and his friends to enjoy."

"Yes *badada*," I said, pulling myself up from the floor and heading towards the kitchen where I would get some plastic plates and tumblers for our foreign visitors.

"Maybe you would like to drink some tea?" my father asked.

"No, thank you. Water is just fine."

"Maybe you would like some *chindongwa*? *Chindongwa* is our traditional drink. It is made from a mixture of maize porridge and millet. Our Chichewa friends call it *thobwa*. It is very delicious."

The visitors hesitated for a few seconds before Alison finally said: "I would like that very much."

I went back and brought the *chindongwa* in individual plastic cups. I also had a bowl of brown sugar and two tablespoons with me. They seemed to like it because they asked me to fetch some more. The Coca-Cola and Fanta arrived a few minutes later but our visitors refused the cold drinks. They said their stomachs were already full.

"Would you like my Fanta?" Alison asked me.

You will never guess how happy I was. I said "yes!" way too quickly, in case she had second thoughts. Derrick wouldn't believe me if I told him that I had drunk a whole Fanta just by myself! My parents helped themselves to Coca-Cola and we took our time, enjoying the sweet elixir to the last drop.

During this time, John told us that he was from Sussex.

"The Duchess of Sussex!" I exclaimed. "I know all about the royal wedding. I read the whole story in the newspaper."

Suddenly, Suzie took out a small object from her backpack. It looked like a miniature TV screen. There was a video recording of the wedding and we all watched it in awe.

"This is a beautiful wedding, *mwe*. Did you go there? What did you eat?" I asked her.

"No, no," Suzie laughed. "I downloaded this video from the Internet."

We didn't understand what she said so we just nodded.

"Why isn't she called a princess? She married a prince, didn't she?"

"She was not born a princess so she cannot be called one."

"Oh," I said. "This is why Kate is called the Duchess of Cambridge."

"Yes, exactly."

"How do you know all these names?" my mother asked, laughing. I just know the Queen and his son Charles. I also used to know late Princess Diana. And when it comes to Africa, I know King Mswati from Swaziland."

"Then you need to catch up on our Royal Family Tree then," Steven said.

While he explained the intricacies of royalty, John went outside to check on the lorry. He came back and said that everything was alright. "There are too many people outside there though. There is too much excitement. Maybe we should get on with our business."

"No, no, no. Sit down young man," my father told him. " Your vehicle is in safe hands. Don't worry."

John sat down but we saw that his mind was elsewhere.

My father asked me to clear the table and reminded me to come back so that I could continue taking down some notes.

After living room was clean, we all sat down and resumed our talk.

"So my dear friends, tell me what is the purpose of your visit." John shifted in his seat and let Alison do the talking.

"Thank you Sir for receiving us in your house. Before leaving England, we saw a documentary about underdeveloped countries."

"Oh," my father said. "Underdeveloped countries? Whoever came up with such a foolish appellation?"

"We could not take our eyes off those poor kids," she said, visibly shaken by her experience in England. "We knew we had to do something. You know when you see such physical and mental distress, you cannot just sit down and do nothing about it. No, you can't. We had to come as soon as the opportunity arose."

"Oh, I feel your pain my daughter," my mother said. " I feel your pain."

"We told ourselves that people shouldn't be living like that in the twenty-first century," Mary added. "We cannot let people live like that in what we call our modern times."

"Oh," my father said. "I understand you."

"So we came up with this idea of raising some funds to buy things for the poor kids here."

My father thought for a moment, his head resting in his right palm. He shook his head and then opened his mouth:

"I understand your concern. It is such an honourable thing to do, to think of other people's pain or suffering. I can see your journey. You left your homes in order to do this. It is an honourable thing to do. Not many people in our own country will do such a thing. Not many people will lift a finger to help a poor child."

"True, true. I agree with you *Dada*," my mother said.

"However, let me tell you something our dear visitors. In our custom, we do not tell an adult that he is wrong in front of a child."

"I agree."

"We do not do such a thing."

"No *Dada*."

"But today will be an exception. Today, I will have to tell you where you have erred my dear visitors. Please do understand that my intention is not to offend you."

"No, we aren't going to be upset," Alison said.

"You know, we can all learn from each other. I can teach you something and you can teach me something.

Knowledge is a two-way process. No man is wiser than another, you understand that, don't you?"

"Yes, we do," Alison and Suzie said.

"No offence," John said.

"*Namaste.*" Steven made a peace sign.

"I have thought about your honourable gesture and I think that it is not a reasonable thing to do. Not at all. If my neighbour sees that my children are crying because of hunger and he gives them a full chicken, do you think that those very children will want to stay in my house when they are fully aware that there is plenty of food just across the road?"

"No, I don't think so. No, I think that your children will want to go to your neighbour's house all the time," John replied.

"I have another question for you John. Don't you have any poor people in your own country?"

"Yes, we do. We do, surely."

"So why didn't you take those things that are in that vehicle to them?"

"The situation seemed more urgent here. I mean the children seemed poorer here. They had no shoes. They looked hungry. Some of them were just staying at home, not going to school."

"Oh, I understand."

My father took off his glasses and put them on again. He thought for some time and then finally asked my mother if she wanted to say something to our visitors.

"I think the children will be happy with what these visitors have brought. I mean, I will never be able to afford whatever things these charitable people have brought," my mother said emphatically.

I agreed with my mother. I didn't even want to think about what my father would do with the objects that were in the lorry outside.

"Well, I have another question for you dear visitors. What will happen when those things that you have brought to us come to an end? You know objects are not eternal. Where will we get the money to replace them? What will my children do if they see that I cannot afford to get them those things anymore? What will they do? Are they going to steal in order to have a taste of that life again?"

John shrugged his shoulders and looked at Steven. The latter said nothing.

"What is in that vehicle?"

Mary explained that they had mostly brought toys and games (dolls, toy soldiers, toy cars, fancy dress costumes, building bricks, puzzles, face painting kits, pretend play sets, styling heads, frisbees, etc). There were also some school bags, some shoes, some clothes and some fairy tale books to read. The more Mary listed the items, the more I became excited. We were finally going to be rich! We would be the envy of the whole village!

"How are you going to distribute those objects? You know, here, when one child has a mango, he shares it with all his friends. This will create a lot of jealous feelings. You think you are coming here to solve problems but in fact, you are a creating new ones. This is irresponsible behaviour."

My mother nodded in agreement. Our visitors did not know what to say.

"I suggest that in the future, if you want to do a similar thing, come and see how we live first. Our needs are very different from yours. What might seem very important to you in England is something that we can live without here and vice-versa."

Alison said: " I understand what you are saying Sir, but it is really difficult for us to see images of children with big bellies staring at us. We have this strong urge to do something to alleviate their suffering. The children look unkempt and it seems like there is no one looking after them. We come with good intentions. Really, nothing else."

"When our kids see that you are giving them free things, they think that there is more from where that came from. They think that you do not have to work in your country in order to earn a living. Do not be surprised when they come rushing at your borders. They think that you have an easy life but I'm sure that you have your own type of suffering. Life is not easy for everyone."

After a lot of debate, we agreed that we had to rethink this whole issue of donations and aid. Our country had been free from colonialism for more than fifty years and we still seemed to be unable to take care of ourselves. The state of our hospitals was awful. Most of our schools were ramshackle buildings with no proper furniture and materials. Our roads were an eyesore. Our children were leaving us in scores, looking for greener pastures elsewhere. We were not economically independent. Complete strangers with no idea of what our culture, aspirations and hope as human beings would not be the ones to come to our rescue. How long would this last? Would Suzie, Steven, Alison and John be there in fifty years' time again? No, this was nonsensical. It was time we pulled up our sleeves to create a safe future for our children and grandchildren. It was time to stop looking for scapegoats.

My mother said she was tired of cooking in a smoky kitchen. She didn't want a cooker, no. There was no electricity in the village. Yet, she wanted a better life, better schools and better hospitals for her children. These were her basic needs. She also wanted to have more time to run a business and be able to look after her children. There were chores that were dreary, boring and repetitive that she didn't want to do anymore: fetching water several times a day, fetching firewood, mending endless clothes, mending the thatched roof, as if there were no qualified engineers in the country! No, she could make better use of her time.

It wasn't Alison's role to save her though. She was the one to save herself. It was her responsibility, she said. It was her responsibility to look after herself. "We do not let our neighbours to come and raise our children," she insisted. "Why do we think strangers that we have never ever seen before will come to solve our problems with objects that we don't really need?" My parents decided that our newly-met friends would take back what they had brought to us. Our family did not need all that. The village did not need all that.

I almost cried. All those toys! All those clothes! All those shoes! Where would they go? It was good for me, he insisted. It was good for us, for everyone. I would understand, he said, I would understand when I became a parent myself.

What a huge disappointment! I didn't want to understand. I wanted those things. I wanted them so bad. After this incident, I did not talk to my father for days. I-mean-for-days. How could he do that? Even my friends could not believe it when they saw the lorry leaving with all those tantalising objects, never to come back. How could your father do such a thing to us? they said. How could he?

"Parents, oh dear parents," I told my mother. "I will never understand them. I will never, ever understand them. Never, ever."

"You will, my dear child," my mother said soothingly but firmly. "You will. Your mother is your mother even if she has one leg. She is still your mother. She is the person who brought you into this world."

The Last Piece of Chicken
(with the Simple Present Tense)

I love chicken.

In my home, we eat chicken with rice once a week. Our mother prepares the meal before we go to church on Sundays. We are very happy when we get back home because we know that the food is already on the table. All we have to do is sit down and enjoy the delicious feast. The problem is that everyone in our family loves chicken.

My father does; my mother does; and even my three year-old-brother does. What I cannot stand is when we fight for the chicken with my elder brother.

He is quicker than I and he often gets the last piece of chicken.

Today is Sunday and I want to outwit him.

First, let me tell you about our daily routine on Sundays. We wake up two hours later than usual. This means that the alarm sounds at eight. My brother and I head straight to the bathroom where we wash our faces and brush our teeth. Then we go back to the bedroom to change into working clothes. These are usually run-down shorts and t-shirts that we are not afraid of soiling. Then, we go to the garden in our plastic slippers and start sweeping the yard.

We make sure that every nook and cranny of the garden is swept carefully because my father always comes to inspect our work afterwards. When we finish, we go to the bathroom once again to wash ourselves. On Sundays, we have the luxury of hot water so we enjoy each and every second of it.

Later, we put on our best clothes. We want to look nice because we meet a lot of people at church and everyone always looks their best. My favourite attire is a grey suit that my father bought in South Africa when he went there for a business trip. My friends say that I look very elegant in that suit and when it is paired with my black leather shoes, it is difficult to recognise me.

Today, I decide to wear this suit because I want to get the last piece of chicken. My father says that when you go for an interview or an important meeting, you should always look the part because you do not want to spoil your chances of getting a job or a contract.

Chuma, my elder brother, does not know that today is my day. Today, I am going to get the contract. I have a plan and this plan will help me get the last piece of chicken.

After church, we arrive home at 1.00 p.m. My mother puts the food on the table. Today we are having a full roasted chicken. There are French fries too! The food smells so good and I cannot wait to get my hands on it. My father takes a knife and cuts the chicken into half.

Pleasant aromas fill the room and I know at that moment that my plan *should* work because I want that last piece of chicken.

We start eating. Once again, I can say that my mother knows how to cook. The meat is not too soft and it is not too hard either. It is just right. The seasoning is nice and I do not even have to add extra salt.

The rice and chicken are very good friends. The French fries are crispy and soft at the same time. The salad is divine. Oh God, the food is so tasty and yummy I almost forget about my plan.

I wake up from my slumber and decide to act on my plan to get the last piece of chicken.

"I have something important to tell you."

Everybody is annoyed because we cannot speak while eating. It is forbidden because no one wants to see what is in our mouths. I apologise very quickly before continuing.

"We can do a quiz at the end of the meal. The one who wins gets the last piece of chicken."

My father stares at me as if I am trying to give him the bad end of a deal. My mother does not need to say anything but there is disapproval on her face. My younger brother keeps on smiling —he is enjoying his food. Chuma stops eating; he is thinking.

"Father will ask the questions. Any type of questions to test our knowledge on what we know about our world." My father smiles and he is followed by my mother. Knowledge is the key to my parents' hearts. Chuma is not happy. My youngest brother grins —he is still enjoying his food.

Chuma senses something.

"Kevin, you're up to something."

My name is Kevin if you don't know me. Well, it is clear to me at this moment that the fight is between Chuma and me. We are both very good at school so this quiz will be a piece of cake for either of us.

"Come on Chuma. Don't chicken out! Just think of the prize. You'll get the last piece of chicken!"

A few seconds go by and Chuma finally decides to do the quiz. My father says that we should wait until there is only one piece of chicken in the plate. He will not participate in the game since he is the umpire. We agree.

When we are finally ready to start, my father stands up. Oh, he likes the drama of dishing out the questions and seeing us stammer with hesitation when we do not know the right answers.

He speaks with a deep voice like his favourite TV presenter.

"Ladies and Gentlemen, welcome to Sunday Quiz. I am your host, Chuma Senior Kumwenda. Our contestants today are Chuma Junior, Kevin, Mary and a three-year-old boy called Trevor because he is clever, ha, ha."

My father likes laughing at his own jokes but we are in no mood to laugh. We want to start the game!

Next, he tells us the rules of the game. We have to raise our right hand when we know the answer. Shouting is prohibited. We should not curse each other, especially since it's our Lord's Day. The person who gets five answers before anyone else is the lucky winner.

Fair enough. We all agree with the rules. Ready, steady, go!

After three minutes, my mother is leading. She knows a lot of things like the exact dates of the fall of the Berlin

Wall and the end of World War II. Well... Chuma and I are mad of course. How can we know all those things? We are not that old! My mother says that we should pay more attention in class.

Then my mother answers the next three questions easily and wins the game! She wins the game!

How can Chuma and I know, let alone young Trevor even though he is clever, how can we know where our current president was born and where he studied at university for the first time? The last question was even worse. "What is the capital city of Chile?" Why father? Why? I don't even know where Chile is!

My father hands the last piece of chicken to my mother. She is beaming with joy and there is the smile of victory on her face. Chuma and I get up from the table but my father tells us to sit down.

"Kevin, this was your idea, wasn't it?" he asks me with concern.

"Yes, it was," I mumble a reply.

"Well, congratulate your mother then. She won fairly."

I tell her what a great person she is, no wonder her children are intelligent too. My mother smiles and starts removing the flesh from the chicken.

"Trevor, do you want some chicken?"

Trevor nods his head and my mother hands him the meat. He is smiling as his fork finds the first piece of chicken. He eats joyfully until there is only one piece left.

"Kevin, do you want some?" Trevor asks me and I smile.

"Of course I do, you little one."

He gives me the last piece of chicken and I pop it into my mouth.

It is as tasty as I'd imagined it.

It is the last piece of chicken after all!

Beyond

(with Airport Vocabulary)

I met him. We didn't talk. I didn't want to. He didn't talk. Mute, Muted, Muted. Tongue-tied, voiceless, speechless. We felt comfortable in the silence. The silence that heals and elevates. The silence that soothes the soulless sores and brings solace to the unanchored soul. The silence in whose bosom we rest. The silence into which we delve in order to find the answers that we seek. The silence that finally yields those answers painstakingly, indirectly, interminably.

He offered to carry my suitcase. It was heavy, I told him. Too heavy for his flail shoulders to carry. We could take the trolley. It was time-saving and practical. This burden, this burden right there, he could avoid it. He had to set his priorities straight. In this life, he had to choose the kind of burdens he wanted to carry.

Therefore, we settled for the trolley. It was convenient, we agreed. It could take us anywhere.

We headed towards the check-in area. It was crowded. There were families. There were single men. There were women clad in bright attires. Children laughed, cried, ran about. The air was rife with excitement.

Our hearts beat with expectation, anticipation. The time had come. We were ready. We were ready to face whatever challenges that would come our way with dignity and pride. We were ready to take on those challenges with courage and determination. We were ready to deal with those challenges with unhampered confidence and belief in a bright future that nurtured our youngest ones and cared for the oldest amongst us. The time had come.

The airline representative was friendly and charming. She answered our questions with incredible patience and know-how. She wished us well as our checked baggage disappeared from sight, carried away by the conveyor belt. We thanked her and acknowledged that the process had been less stressful than we had previously imagined.

We braced ourselves for the passport control process. We prepared answers to questions we didn't know. We checked our carry-on luggage to see if there were things that were not supposed to be there. We threw away water or whatever thing that would appear suspicious to the eyes of those whose sole and unique stamp could put a lid on fifteen years of unquenchable dreams. Our tongues became stale. We walked on with laboured breathing, one foot after another.

There were two queues. We instinctively took the one that was meant for us. We asked ourselves why we tolerated this when we had paid the same price for the air ticket. We vowed to ourselves that this would be the last time we would be undergoing such treatment. Our hard work and prosperity would speak for us. Our dignity as human beings would be returned by the sweat of our brows. Our worth would be validated by the wealth of our hands, hearts and minds. Desperation wasn't an option, no. Desperation wasn't an option for us.

The questioning lasted two hours. Two whole hours of too much questioning. Where were we going? Why were we going there? How were we going there? What were we going to do there? Whom were we going to live with? How much money did we have? When were we planning to go back? Did we want to work? Were we going to get married? Were we going to have children? Gosh, it seemed their tongues would break loose and run away from the incessant battering, but we held on, we held on, we held on. We stood firm and we answered those relentless questions, repeatedly, courageously, thoroughly. We showed our passports, our boarding passes, our school admission letters, our affidavits of birth or birth certificates. Everything. We took everything that would convince the immigration officers that we were just students who wanted to get better opportunities elsewhere. Stop the nonsense. We wanted to work hard, damn it! We didn't want anything else, my, my, my. We sighed from exhaustion and frustration, but we never faltered. We never did.

They finally relented and let us through. We went past the security check in a shaken state but we did not fall because we knew what we were made of. We understood very well, really well, that our stay would be difficult but we'd make the most of those years, we promised ourselves. Those years wouldn't be wasted, no. This hassle, this senseless hassle of trying to go to places where we didn't belong wasn't worth our time. Not anymore, not anymore.

What if we spent the same enormous energy building the universities that we lacked in our communities? we asked ourselves. What if we turned this destructive energy into creative energy that would transform our villages into safe havens? What if, what if, instead of walking a thousand miles to a place we didn't know, we built roads that would lead us to an incredible future? What if, what if, we stopped drowning in unknown salty and murky waters and held on to our lives? These lives-those lives-so precious, valuable, priceless, irreplaceable! What if...We thought about all those things as we boarded the plane that was taking us to unfamiliar surroundings and faces.

When the plane took off, we held our hands firmly and looked around us. We knew. We knew right then, in our silence, that the sky wasn't the limit for us. We could touch it, right there, serenely, and never let it go. Not in this lifetime!

THE END

www.ingramcontent.com/pod-product-compliance
Lightning Source LLC
LaVergne TN
LVHW091621170726
843492LV00007B/2544